RENDEZVOUS WITH A STUDENT'S DREAM

RAJESH KUMAR SARAOGI
ACA, ACMA, ACS, LLB (GEN.)

Edition 2017

Published in India by Zorba Books, 2017
Website: www.zorbabooks.com
Email: info@zorbabooks.com

ISBN Print book (paperback): 978- 93- 5267-329- 2
ISBN Print book (hardcover): 978- 93- 5267-330- 8
ISBN E- book: 978- 93- 5267-328- 5
(All ISBN in Author's name)

Zorba Books Pvt. Ltd. (opc)
Gurgaon, INDIA

Printed at : Repro Knowledgecast Limited, Thane

Living Life with positive energy

I dedicate this book to my parents, family, colleagues and all my friends, who inspired me to write down my thoughts as a guide for millions of students around the world and to share the experiences I've gathered over the last twenty-five years.

Book cover Artist: SelfPubBookCovers.com/RLSather

Table of Contents

Personal note from the author

Rendezvous with a Student's Dream is a compilation of short essays based on true experiences, intended to inspire leadership qualities and give individuals the internal strength to meet daily challenges, face reality in every sphere of life, achieve their goals and obtain happiness through positive energy.

Every individual has different career goals and is a student in some way throughout his life; everyone learns from his own experiences how to achieve his aspirations and goals.

I have shared my experiences in each chapter of the book, narrating the different phases an individual experiences in the 'journey of life', from childhood to old age and finally retirement.

Everyone knows that the future is uncertain, and this uncertainty creates fear in the minds of millions of people around the world. They doubt whether they will be successful and make the right crucial decisions in various stages of life, be it as a leader of a country, a successful professional, a businessman, a student or a housewife.

I have experienced various crisis situations in life, such as the reality of living in fear during Saddam Hussein's invasion of Kuwait or the fear of death during Cyclone Gonu, which took lives, destroyed property and disrupted many more lives in Oman.

I have also become unemployed due to ideological differences on many occasions while going up the ladder of life. However, every crisis, calamity and disaster in my life opened new horizons and strengthened me to face the fear within.

Every door which has closed in my life led to the opening of a new door that, in the end, improved my quality of life. This has inspired me to write about my experiences.

Every person reading this compilation, whether a student or a successful businessman, a professional or a leader, knows that fear of failure is a normal phenomenon before making a decision at any stage of life, be it choosing a course of education, starting a new job or beginning a new business venture.

Rendezvous with a Student's Dream is a must-read for young students who want to overcome the failures in life and achieve their goals in this competitive and materialistic world, where everyone runs around without realizing how, why or where!

For more information, visit Rajesh Kumar Saraogi's profile on Linked-in or his website, www.strategytolead.com

CHAPTER 1

Expectations from others over the years develop unconscious fear and doubt in an individual's mind about his ability to achieve his career goals and expectations in life.

From the day a child is born, parents have expectations for him: they expect their children to start walking early, to start talking early, to start eating solid food, to go to school early, to get good marks, to achieve his dreams and so on. Over time, these expectations put pressure and eventually fear in the child's mind—the fear of not being able to meet his parents' expectations or of not being able to achieve his own goals. From the time a child begins school, every parent starts to dream that one day their son or daughter will become an engineer or a doctor, a chartered accountant or a business owner, and then the pressure starts: coaching classes, extra classes, etc., to ensure that the child passes with flying colours. And this pressure in turn causes the fear of failure to grow in the child's mind from the earliest stages of his life.

However, expectation is life, and a life without expectations has nothing to look forward to, so balancing expectations is what life is all about. It is normal for humans to expect things from each other. If parents have too few hopes for their children, this can cause the children to miss opportunities and create a negative aura. At the same time, hopes that are too high are also difficult to handle, especially if the child doesn't fulfil their parents' hopes. Sometimes, the failure to meet expectations and the fear and pressure that go with them has driven individuals to depression or even suicide.

The best way to meet others' expectations is to balance them and take them as they come rather than focusing on them and creating negative energy around them.

CHAPTER 2

Family and parents have a very strong influence on an individual in the early stages of life and career.

From childhood to adolescence to adulthood, family and parents play a very important role in an individual's life, and a child's destiny is shaped by the strength his family gives him, affecting how he faces the challenges of the various stages of life.

At the beginning of an individual's career, he needs strong moral support from his parents. This starts in childhood and continues through his early education until he finally comes face to face with the wide world. A child's family and parents can change his destiny if they use their own experience to guide him from time to time so he can handle growing up and facing the day-to-day challenges of the competitive environment that is life. A person's childhood shapes his future when he becomes an adult. A child who is given positive support and encouragement becomes a successful individual and, in the end, has the satisfaction of having led a good life.

Culture, tradition, society and family values are the fundamental foundations for guidance in life.

No individual is born good or bad, but culture, traditions and fundamental family roots shape an individual's perception of life as he grows, and that defines right and wrong for him. Therefore, it is very important for young children to have a strong foundation, which comes from family guidance, culture and traditions and human values. Punishment at later stages in life cannot change the perceptions formed by childhood experiences, and negative influences always leave a scar cannot easily heal, even as the years of life roll by.

CHAPTER 3

Education is only a way to gain knowledge; it is practical experience that assists one to achieve his career goals.

Education gives knowledge, but knowledge without practical experience has no value. Many successful individuals have gained practical experience that enabled them to achieve their goals, even though they did not have the opportunity for a formal education. Their real education was their experience. However, that certainly does not mean that formal education is unnecessary, but it is only one of the possible paths to success.

Education is a tool for achieving one's goals. Most people who are educated are averse to taking risks and end up working for those who do take risks, who may or may not be highly educated.

So it is important to decide on one's goal: do you want to be a business owner—and do you have the entrepreneurial skills to take risks—or do you want to work for someone else? This is the burning question that decides an individual's future.

Risk and rewards always go hand in hand, and to achieve any goal, one must find a balance without sacrificing ethics or moral values. Money is necessary for life, but living happily does not always mean more money.

Education without experience is like a pen without ink; it cannot write. Education gives an individual an initial platform for starting a career, and it can give him a measure of security. However, in the long term, it is a person's life experiences and choices that determine his success in achieving his goals.

CHAPTER 4

Selection of the right career is essential.

No study track is good or bad: the course of study one selects is only the beginning of his career and the stepping stone for future achievements, provided this selection is made thoughtfully, taking one's strengths and weaknesses into account, and not based on friends' aspirations or parents' expectations or dreams.

In the early 1980s, when my colleague Vijay was in the ninth class, all his friends took science or math. He was told that he was good at accounting and commerce and should choose a track focusing on these courses, which in those days was considered an easy option. He took this advice.

Many of Vijay's friends were very good at sports but not at their studies, and their parents used to tell them they would become clerks or be unemployed. But in reality, Vijay watched many of those colleagues grow up to scale new heights in life in many areas—including sports—even though they were never good at their studies.

World-class cricketers such as M.S. Dhoni or Sachin Tendulkar are classic examples of people who achieved their goals in life despite a humble beginning.

As the years passed, Vijay realized that no study track is good or bad. Each individual should look at his own strengths and interests and choose tracks that maximize his strengths in order to do well in life. The fear that came from not doing what others considered the best course slowly faded from Vijay's life as he realized that he had chosen what he was good at and this was proven in his life in later years.

Your belief in yourself is your strength, and that gives you the energy to scale new heights in life, to build skyscrapers, huge ships, space stations or rockets, to land on the moon, to cross new boundaries in research or medicine and to make the world a better place to live.

Once a student starts believing in himself, he knows his strengths and can predict his exam marks and which universities will accept him. As time passes, the fear of not achieving goals slowly vanishes. This fear of failure only stays with students who do not wish to face the realities of life.

Eventually, the time comes in every student's life to think about attending university. He must then start the rigorous task of identifying which university or college to attend, what to study, where to go, whether he will be accepted, etc. All this uncertainty about the future can strike fear in a student's mind: will he get into a good college or university? What should he study?

In today's competitive world, it is better to take academic courses that interest you and have a practical focus, rather than only theoretical courses, which in many cases provide an education but do not lead to employment. One should select courses that give him the opportunity to excel and to become a bread-winner at an early age, which in turn will make him a confident player in life.

There are many practical courses of study, and they can lead to such diverse careers as that of a pilot, a naval officer, an army officer, a nurse, an athlete, a musician, a dancer, a software developer, a specialist mechanic or a heavy equipment driver. These are in addition to the most popular careers: doctor, engineer, and accountant or IAS officer. Since most students want to pursue such careers and the majority seek to, such programs are always competitive, and one should be prepared to face this fact. Therefore, the choice of a course of study should be based on one's strengths and interests.

Furthermore, on completing any degree or diploma, one should not have to ask himself what to do next or if the next step will be unemployment; this kind of frustration just makes life difficult. Therefore, after completing a course of study, the student should know exactly what his next course of action in his career should be, and he should know the next steps towards his goals.

Talents and skills which are scarce are in high demand in any society and can always lead to income opportunities, whether through entrepreneurship or in another way.

CHAPTER 5

Recognize and identify your strengths and believe in yourself, and you will achieve your career goals.

In school and college, students are very ambitious and aggressive, and they often believe that after their studies, life will settle down and their dreams of success and luxury will be automatically achieved once they pass their examinations. The reality of life is that the best years of life are the years of study in school and college, and once they are over, real life begins, and the struggle for success begins with it.

This creates new fears in an individual's mind: what company to join, what position to pursue, etc. Clearly, the constant uncertainties in life create fear that one won't achieve his goals. This fear can drive many students to depression or suicide, but that can be avoided if they believe in themselves and recognize their true strengths.

God has given every person specific abilities and strengths and special qualities, and each person must identify these for himself. The moment he does that, his life becomes satisfying at every stage, and the fear of failure slowly evaporates.

World history is full of great individuals who were ordinary people, such as Abraham Lincoln, Gandhi and many other great leaders who believed in themselves and were able to achieve challenging goals after many uncertainties and failures in life. They believed in their strengths and therefore could overcome their weaknesses at every stage of life and become a beacon for others.

CHAPTER 6

Peers, colleagues and supervisors at work have a very strong influence on an individual's career goals.

After an individual leaves his family and begins working in an organization or company, often in a new city or location, the opinions of his peers and colleagues have a very big impact on his career goals. Many individuals are very influenced by their colleagues and their friends and compare themselves with them, which can lead to substantial dissatisfaction and shallow competition, resulting in hurt egos and jealousy. The influence of peers can even destroy an individual when it guides him in the wrong direction, as it will if he tries to copy his peers without understanding his own strengths. This will cause him to make poor decisions, which he will repent later when he has failed to achieve what he wanted. Therefore, every individual needs to understand his own strengths and weakness and choose his life path accordingly.

Positive influence from peers can substantially shape an individual's career, and most organizations are successful thanks to positive individuals in the organization who believe in teamwork rather than individual performance. Organizations are nothing but people, and leaders who think differently and believe in their ideas can direct and shape the future of an organization and the destiny of is people.

It is human capital that shapes the future, not machines. Microsoft, Google and Facebook are 21st-century examples: they were invented by human leaders, and they have each revolutionized society and industry and have changed the world in many spheres of life.

Companies and countries, too, are led by individuals whose positive thoughts give them the inherent strength to influence others and change the world to make it a better place for everyone.

My colleague Vijay was friends with some of the most brilliant, high-scoring students in his class, and these excellent peers gave him guidance but also taught him some of their skills, which eventually helped him to achieve his career goals.

CHAPTER 7

Set objectives and goals in life and work for them step by step; there are no short cuts or easy ways to achieve them.

Every individual must have goals; this gives meaning and purpose to life. These goals should take one's strengths and weakness into account by writing them down in a SWOT analysis, making sure that the goals are realistic.

The goals can be personal, so one can constantly compare his achievements against the overall target and measure his progress. Constant improvement, as measured by progress towards a self-selected target, gives a person immense mental satisfaction as he sees how much better he is now than in the past—in every respect. Once set in motion, this process of improvement leads to a lifelong competition with one's own self, rather than with anyone else. This results in a more focused approach to life than comparing oneself with others, which only leads to dissatisfaction and depression.

Therefore, everyone should have his own scale of measurement to evaluate his achievements, rather than comparing himself with colleagues and friends. This is the key to satisfaction in life. The aim should be to become better than one was in the past, not better than anyone else.

Worrying about problems does not solve anything or achieve any goals, but constant planning as to how to achieve them produces the desired results.

The achievement of goals depends on an individual's vision and ability to believe in himself, and every failure should strengthen his beliefs rather than weaken them.

CHAPTER 8

A positive approach makes even the most difficult goals easy to achieve.

Often, when a person is near a goal, he suddenly gets a shock and finds that what was so near to success has suddenly become a failure. This can start a cycle of negative thinking. However, such events are a test. At such a time, one needs to look at life positively and challenge himself to work even harder to achieve his goals. This will make him stronger and more confident. What is destruction for one is an opportunity for another, so the way one responds to such events makes one successful in life or not.

When Vijay was in Kuwait in 1990 during the Gulf War, what kept him alive was his positive attitude—the belief that he could survive and the will to do so. This enabled him and many others to return to their home countries in spite of all the obstacles and difficulties they faced.

The world is always changing. It is full of new ideas, new hopes and new goals, and the positive approach is the only way for a person to meet his goals and make the world a better place, not only for himself but for all human beings.

Many times in life, a person becomes very negative due to constant failures and starts to lose confidence. This can lead to the beginning of depression and create a strong aura of negative energy, which can only be destroyed by the positive energy of a mentor who can guide the individual through such a situation.

Vijay was always very positive about his life, and consistent study, along with sincere effort and belief in his abilities, enabled him to pass the tough chartered accountancy exams and obtain the professional qualification that was his career goal. This positive approach helped Vijay handle difficult situations and become more successful in the following years.

Wait patiently for the right time to take advantage of opportunities.

Sometimes it is important to wait patiently for the right opportunity. Life gives many opportunities to everyone, but what is important is to take the right opportunity for your own goals. Opportunities taken decide one's fate in the future.

CHAPTER 9

Believe in destiny but do not be ruled by it; there is no alternative to Karma, i.e., Work.

They say that every act in life is pre-written by an unknown power. If this is true, it is not helpful to focus only on results; just act positively and the results will follow.

Sometimes the results are not what one anticipates, and the only way to meet one's aspirations and expectations is to continue to be positive and work towards them.

Negative people create negative thoughts, but positive people create positive thoughts. So it is important to be with positive people to achieve one's goals through hard work and perseverance.

Many people in the world believe in destiny and try to pass off any failure in life as destiny, but it is a person's actions that decide his destiny.

Respect every individual, rich or poor, as the positive energy from their wishes create goodwill and form your reputation.

It is very important to respect every individual's view, be they rich or poor, and adopt opinions that create positive energy. This will automatically lead to goodwill and a good reputation of sound judgment.

Over the years, Vijay learned that success is a team effort and that the least important individuals in an organization need respect in order for the organization to be strong and successful. So, as he rose to leadership in his company, Vijay spent a lot of his time listening to employees' personal problems and trying understanding the fabric of the organization. So the employees began to trust him, and then they obeyed his orders because they respected those orders and the person giving them.

A leader can never learn the true facts sitting alone in an office or at home. He must personally interact with his people and his team and understand the complex processes that make the organization work in order to take it to new heights.

CHAPTER 10

Collect all the facts and be a good listener to make good decisions.

It is important to be a good listener and collect all the facts before making any decision. Once a leader has the perspectives of all the people involved in the decision, he can make the correct decision.

Making decisions in a hurry, without all the facts, is the main cause of poor decisions, which lead to the failure of individuals, projects and organizations. Incomplete or wrong information can lead to wrong decisions.

Therefore, the only way to make a good decision is with all the facts. This requires interacting with people and patiently listening to them. Patience is one of the keys to success.

Keep a 'to do' list as a constant reminder and follow up regularly.

Every individual needs to keep a diary and write down his life goals and his plans for achieving them. He should also write down every decision and step towards these goals as a basis for future decisions. Then he can later remember that every decision took the current circumstances into account, so he will have no cause for repentance.

Most people say that if they had the opportunity they would do things differently. However, the fact is that every decision is made with reference to a particular situation, and when the situation changes, the right decisions also change from time to time.

No decision is perfect, but sometimes the most important thing is simply to make a choice—although not making a decision can be a choice as well—and all of an individual's choices and actions determine his fate and the goals he will achieve.

CHAPTER 11

Life is nothing but building relationships — good and bad relationships affect your goals.

Life goals are not achieved through money. Instead, build relationships and trust, and money will follow. The more relationships an individual develops, the more opportunities he has, and this ultimately leads to success. Networking is very important, but at the same time, it must be the right networking in order to reap the benefits. Building relationships and networking are the mantras of successful people. As one becomes more successful, he comes across all kinds of people, and relationships that make one happy and successful as the years roll by are a treasure.

Good relationships create positive energy, but bad relationships lead to jealousy and competition. When an individual has bad relationships, he starts spending more time sorting them out than focusing on his goals. He may delay or fail to achieve his goals in the end due to this loss of focus.

Take every opportunity to develop relationships and network through the internet, media and travel, but personal contact is the only way to develop long-term relationships.

There are many ways to develop relationships in today's digital world, but face-to-face contact is still the best way to build a strong and lasting relationship.

Connections and contacts can always lead to opportunities for career growth, but one needs to sense these opportunities as they occur. Opportunities for personal contacts come when a person attends social and professional functions, seminars, and professional trainings or courses and so on; opportunities to reach your goals also occur when one meets new people from different professions and industries.

Most people who reach their goals do so because they had the opportunity to meet successful people who guided them and gave them the opportunity to achieve their dreams. The earlier a person realizes that building relationships is the foundation of success, the faster he can progress in his career towards his goals.

Try to make your individual goals a part of your organization's or team's goals as well; this synchronization will result in a win-win situation.

CHAPTER 12

To walk the ladder of success, know your weaknesses and accept them publicly so that you can move forward with a new beginning.

They say that to protect one lie you need to tell a hundred more lies and the final result is still negative. Therefore, it is always better to be upfront and face and accept the facts rather than try to avoid them or blame someone else for one's own actions. This honest approach makes life easier, and a new beginning is possible at any time.

Most individuals like to hide the truth and are unable to face facts. They constantly find excuses to justify their own actions. Unknowingly, they damage themselves with this thought process; they need to find, correct and amend their mistakes as quickly as possible to move forward.

Be a leader and a team player; select a team of leaders and not followers, and believe in their ability to perform.

A leader is one who leads by example, so never ask others to do what you are not willing to do yourself. Due to their own insecurities, most people would rather lead a team of followers than a team of leaders. A team of followers can only do what you want or tell them to do, whether right or wrong. They won't express their own opinions. However, strong individuals with leadership qualities express their true opinions without any fear, which makes them stand out from others and gives them the strength to take the team forward. People who are followers simply follow the BOSS's orders. They are not true team players but are opportunists waiting to pull the BOSS down if he fails. When there are problems, they have excuses: 'I wasn't consulted', 'I didn't have time', 'I didn't know', etc. The real truth is that when one has the best people on a team—a team of leaders—then one scores a goal.

Therefore, to reach new heights, every member of a team should have leadership qualities and be able to challenge the leader on every decision. Then the leader knows all the pros and cons of a choice and is prepared to face the challenges and overcome them. While a leader is the final decision maker, the team's involvement in the decision-making process makes them more responsible and lets the leader look at problems from a different angle. This approach also creates various options and solutions for obstacles and failures, which can happen when any decision is made.

CHAPTER 13

Failures are the stepping stones to success; identify the causes and correct them rather than taking a negative approach.

Most of us always view failure as a negative thing, without realizing that unless there are failures, there is no success. Every failure is a new learning experience and a way to move forward in life. History is full of stories of people who failed at first and later, with consistent hard work, overcame their failures and become example for others. Bill Gates is one of the leading examples of the century; he created revolutionary change in world with his success.

Vijay often worried about the fact that, despite his good education, the early years of his career did not enable him to obtain the luxuries he wanted. However, as the years went by, he became more and more experienced and successful and progressed in his career. Every failure taught him a new way to overcome problems. Today, when he looks back at his life, he knows that it was only through hard work and consistently accepting and correcting his mistakes that he achieved what he desired.

Constant struggle in life is an indication of constant change.

Every failure leads to new struggles, and everyone must constantly upgrade their knowledge and way of thinking on order to face changes. Looking at change positively is the only way to move forward in life and accept new challenges with excitement rather than dwelling in the past and spoiling the future with worry.

Everyone in the world has experienced failure at some point, and it is this struggle to survive which strengthens an individual to face the constant process of change in life.

No amount of wealth can buy time, so time is the most precious thing we all have. We all must live life every day with a positive attitude and face struggles as they come to come out happy and successful and achieve our goals.

Many times, by the time a person achieves success, he is exhausted physically and mentally, and that adversely affects his body and spirit, resulting in the beginning of physical ailments. The entire process of having achieved success becomes meaningless when one is unable to enjoy life.

Every individual should know his own level of endurance and how far he can push himself, and he should avoid reaching beyond his capabilities to avoid irreversible damage to his goals. Time lost can never be regained and the clock of life can never be reversed, so time spent with good health and happiness is true success in life.

CHAPTER 14

Do not express your differences or disagreements by publicly insulting someone; when you disagree with someone, speak with him alone after a lapse of time and you will succeed in convincing him.

It is important to be honest and express one's views, but protocol is also important in order to avoid ego clashes. So it is always advisable to give contrary opinions in private rather than in public, which may insult the person one is contradicting. Many times, a correct opinion given at the wrong time creates bad feelings and negative energy that can become difficult to handle over time. Contradicting a leader on the spur of the moment, even if the leader is wrong, could lead to complications and breed negative energy.

There is nothing wrong with disagreeing with a leader and expressing that opinion. Sometimes good leaders change their opinions when they see a new perspective on a problem, if this perspective is explained in private. Wait a little while (preferably 24 hours) before giving a leader a contrary opinion, as the chances of the new opinion being accepted will be much higher.

Express your true opinions, but agree to disagree when there is a stalemate on a decision, and accept the decision of the individual who has the responsibility and power to make that decision. Sometimes whether a decision is right or wrong is less important than relying on the leader's experience.

Never challenge anyone only to build up your own ego. Most individuals are driven by false ego, and rather than accept the truth, they hide behind false arguments and excuses. This leads to mental disturbances, loss of peace and wasted time and energy that could be spent on their goals. There can only be one leader in a team, and it is his ability to lead, make tough decisions and support the team through challenging situations that earns him the right to lead others.

A skill's scarcity is a key factor determining its financial valuation at a particular time. This process is based on the supply and demand of skills in the market, and it is constantly changing. The scarcity of a person's skills and the value he adds to them decide his value in the market, which gives him the opportunity to lead or be selected for opportunities.

CHAPTER 15

Do not be lost in the materialistic world and join the race to the top, as reaching the top is difficult but remaining there is an even more difficult balancing act.

They say that every goal, once achieved, leads to a new goal. An employee wants to keep moving forward in his career, and a business-man want to keep accumulating wealth, and that is a never-ending story. Real life is about knowing what one wants and whether one has achieved that.

It is difficult to reach the top position as the pyramid narrows at the top and becomes more and more competitive, but it is even more difficult to remain at the top due to people who want to come up pulling you down.

A balancing act is required: thc person at the top of the pyramid in an organization must constantly evaluate whether he should remain there or to let another take that position and move to another organization.

CHAPTER 16

Every individual asks, 'Have I achieved enough in life?' and 'What do I want in life?' Winners are common individuals who have a burning desire in their hearts to achieve their goals.

In today's materialistic world, every individual wants to get ahead. However, success comes to people who have the fire in their bellies to take on new challenges and the burning desire to keep working until they achieve their goals. There is no alternative to hard work and, at the same time, staying vigilant so one can grab opportunities before they pass by to others.

One's actions and decisions at every stage of life determine the results as one goes through the journey of life. If you plant a banana tree, obviously, you will get bananas and not mangoes. So it is important to decide early in life whether you want bananas or mangoes!

Today, Vijay has achieved everything in life that he wanted, but he still wants more and more material things, and his constantly moving goal posts require him to work very hard. This can lead to stress and may finally result in a heart attack, paralysis or some other medical condition, unless he evaluates himself and accepts his limitations.

One needs to know when to stop being ambitious and be satisfied with one's achievements before the frustration and fear of failing to meet constantly changing definitions of success lead to self-annihilation.

Successful people are those who believed that their consistent hard work would enable them to achieve their goals. They measured their achievements against their own benchmarks rather than comparing themselves to others. Comparison with others only breeds jealousy and hatred, which not only destroy the individual but lead to an aimless and frustrating life.

CHAPTER 17

Success and satisfaction are a state of mind, and every step forward should be compared to what you have achieved in the past, rather than to other individuals.

Success in life is defined not by what one has achieved as compared to others but by what one has achieved in the present compared to the past. Comparison breeds jealousy and creates negative energy that makes life difficult. Living with the constant urge to act can lead to an individual's downfall.

Satisfaction is a state of mind, and a person must constantly remind himself to compare his success to where he was a year ago, so that he knows that he is moving up the ladder of success according to his own bench marks.

Real success is the happiness of having led life the way one wants to live and not the way one is forced to live. Many people in the world are not lucky enough to decide what they want; they are forced to do what they don't want by circumstances or other causes.

We all have our fears before achieving our goals, but the bigger challenge is to remain on top after achieving them and to keep setting new milestones to meet the expectations of others—parents, teachers, employers, shareholders or society. Patience, tolerance, consistent hard work and a positive approach are the keys to achieving success and overcoming our fears, which are normal and experienced by every human being in life.

Life is a miracle, a gift of God to mankind, and once a person realizes this truth, he starts living every moment of his life with passion and satisfaction. A student's dream can become reality only if he works towards it passionately, believes in it and pursues it wholeheartedly until he achieves it.

Know when to retire and reap the rewards of your hard work.

They say that no amount of wealth can buy health, so it is important to enjoy the benefits of success by taking breaks from time to time, No one can work constantly, and anyone who tries to will suddenly collapse one fine day from a heart attack or some other ailment.

All individuals age with time and should accept this harsh reality. They need to know when to retire and stop chasing materialistic goals.

When one has achieved his goals in life, it is important to plan a new strategy for living a happy life, keeping in mind one's physical limitations and age constraints. Then he can not only enjoy what he has built over the years but also consider contributing back to society in one form or other, without any expectation of return.

My colleague Vijay, having achieved his career goal as a successful businessman, is now happy and contented in his retirement.

He is giving back to society by mentoring and teaching young students, something he always wanted to do.

In this way, retirement can give an individual immense happiness and satisfaction as he pursues these new goals and ages gracefully.

About the Author

RAJESH KUMAR SARAOGI studied commerce and graduated with honours from Sydenham College, Mumbai University. He has an excellent academic record and holds many professional qualifications, such as ACA, ACMA, ACS and LLB (Gen), obtained in his mid-twenties.

He spent more than twenty-five years of his career in various senior executive positions with large, reputable organizations in India such as Grasim Industries Ltd., Hindustan Motors Ltd., Essar Shipping Ltd., etc., and in the Middle East with companies such as Oman Textiles Mills SAOG, Al Khaleej Polypropylene SAOG, Tiffany Foods Ltd., Shanfari Group of Companies LLC. He is currently a director at

Steamtech & Co. LLC, a specialized oil field services company in the Sultanate of Oman.

He has travelled globally and has deep insight into the business needs of different organizations in a range of industries, including manufacturing, shipping, hospitality, logistics, real estate, travel, automotive, construction, contracting and oil and gas.

He has vast experience in developing business strategies for improving the top and bottom line of any organization through an in-depth study of the business environment.

He also has experience in managing all areas of business and has had the opportunity to be a part of developing many large manufacturing organizations in India and Oman from inception to commissioning. He has core competencies in business strategy, restructuring and organizational turnaround.

The author has faced the harsh realities of life, having experienced the Gulf War in Kuwait and Cyclone Gonu in Oman. Such experiences have given him the strength to overcome his fears and achieve a successful career.

The author comes from a middle class family and was able to achieve his career goals through education, hard work, sincerity and an honest approach to life. He has shared his life experiences through this book.

www.ingramcontent.com/pod-product-compliance
Ingram Content Group UK Ltd.
Pitfield, Milton Keynes, MK11 3LW, UK
UKHW021934190726
13853UKWH00004B/1443

9 789352 673292